D1575174

This book is for

_____

All my *Love,*

_____

you're the best friend ever

you're the best *friend* ever

ellen jacob

**Andrews McMeel
Publishing**

Kansas City

02 03 04 05 QUF 10 9 8 7 6 5 4 3 2

ISBN: 0-7407-1889-4

Library of Congress Catalog Card Number: 2001086853

For my best friend, Leslie.
Your warm heart and great ear are my anchor.
May we talk daily and be friends forever.

Thanks to My Friends

*M*y friends, current and past, made this book possible. My best friend, Leslie, who always listens and shares her wisdom and her heart, helped me understand our friendship and friendship itself. Thanks for listening and sharing and being my friend. Also, thanks to my friend Zanne, who has taught me that you don't need to speak every day to be close. Your perspective and wisdom have gotten me through more than one mishap. And to my best friend of all, my husband, Kirk. Once again your love, support, humor, and funny faces, as well as your helpful edits, kept me on track.

Many thanks to the great team at Andrews McMeel—Kelly Gilbert, Julie Barnes, Christi Clemons Hoffman, and all the others. Thanks for your dedication to this project.

And to my friend Evan Levy, who embraced this project by interviewing countless friends of hers to be included. Also, many thanks to Gwen Gürkan, who, with the background sounds of her new baby, gave her time, talent, and beautiful designs to this book. And to Paulo Duarte, who always pitches in and helps. And to Sherri Phillips and Christina Lambert Clarke, who also contributed their friends' stories as well as their friendship. Thanks, all, for your help and friendship.

Friendship? Yes, please.

——CHARLES DICKENS

The *Inexplicable* Bond

My friends are all very special to me. I count on them, being more aware of them in times of crisis. But the small daily rituals are what makes their friendship so meaningful. We shop together and gab together. We share stories, we give advice. We give and give and get so much more in return.

As a child, my best friend, Paula, and I played together, believing there was no one else who understood us the way we understood each other. We had a secret society and felt we could conquer the world. I learned early the importance of the bonds of friendship. As an adult, the ties are just as strong, just as deep and important, and just as meaningful. As I say elsewhere in this book—it's too big a world to take on alone. Two against the universe is vastly better odds, and loads more fun, than one.

My friend Leslie introduced me to my husband, Kirk—he had bought her company for his company, and I had just started my own company. Leslie set up a business meeting for us all to see if we could work together. Well, we tried work, but what really worked out was Kirk and me! My friend Zanne held my hand through the toughest period of my life. My friend Katherine and I gossiped about dates. Pegi and I work together and take it all in stride. Some of these friend-ships are closer than others, but they all share the common element of an inexplicable bond that enhances my life.

The women and men on the following pages share similar experiences in their friendships. Often, the details are different. But what remains the same is the deep, intimate, mysterious bond that tells us who our friends are. Friends make life's journey possible and wonderful. What an honor it is to be someone's friend.

Friends are those people we choose to create a special bond with and choose to share our lives with. This book is a tribute to all my friends and to friends everywhere. Because, actually, all our friends are the best friends ever.

To write a book on best friends, you have to have one. Leslie is mine. So I start with her—in the same way that I dedicated this book to her. Leslie's story sets the scene for all the other stories of all the true friends who speak through this book.

Questioning *Authority*

*T*OOK THE '70s, AND ALL THEY HAD TO OFFER, VERY SERIOUSLY. At that time, the motto "Question Authority" was on everything from T-shirts to bumper stickers. It summed up what I had been doing since I was first told to take out the garbage.

It was that statement that ultimately drove how I picked my friends. If my friends did not have the basic instinct to question authority, systems, laws, and all institutions, we had little in common. You didn't have to be a renegade, refuse to pay taxes, or have bad hygiene; it just meant that one should question the status quo.

My best friend is Ellen. She is the poster child for New York City. Ellen talks fast, walks fast, thinks fast, and runs fast. And she "gets it" fast on any subject, any problem, anytime.

Our daily conversations range from Bill Clinton to on-the-job politics, from shoes to our mothers' backgrounds in search of reasons for forgiveness, from gun control to why headhunters suck.

This may seem ordinary, but with Ellen and me they happen in about eight- to twelve-minute snippets on cell phones, and not in any particular order, chronological or logical.

> *We were fast friends from that first moment and always have been.*
>
> —LESLIE SINGER

Ellen is usually walking down Broadway or parking her car ("hold on, I just have to make this turn . . ."), or at Kinkos in the middle of a transaction of some kind ("hold on, I just have to get some change out—no black spiral please—hold on, Les, I just dropped my purse—no sir, the line starts over here—still there, Les?").

Many times these conversations get very deep—girl stuff, mom stuff, and hormone stuff. It's the bouncing from one topic to another, from laughing to spilling our guts, from money to clothes, that's exciting. We can disagree, debate, and be inquisitive together. Ellen always gives me real answers, a direct point of view, and an observation. It's rich stuff.

And it's comforting to know that in a pinch, I can ring her on her cell phone. No hello-how-was-your-day kind of stuff. No, you just jump in headfirst into:

Leslie (in a whisper): El, it's me. Listen, I gave a verbal okay to a printer, but now the client has recommended their own printer, but I already have incurred costs, and I didn't get three bids, which is the corporate policy, and the conference call is in ten minutes, and . . .

Ellen (lots of static): Hi, hold on, I'm in Starbucks—Yeah, a latte, please, and can you put in extra chocolate? Sometimes you guys go a little light—hi, yeah, well, I just think you apologize to the printer, tell him the truth, and maybe he hasn't incurred as many costs as you had thought, and hold on—how much? These lattes are very expensive—so, yeah, you know, Les, it's most likely no big deal. And this three-bid thing, we all know it's all bulls----. And anyway, hold on, I'm just opening the door, you can make it up to the printer on the next—oh, hold on . . .

Ellen and I met in an interview. She was a potential client of my design firm. We were fast friends from that first moment and always have been. She's talented, colorful, opinionated, passionate, and a damn good writer and art director. She has more style in her little finger than most people have in their whole being, and always is there when you need a shoulder or an answer. She is there at midnight (which is early) and there at 6 A.M. (she'd been up since 4).

She eats way too many M&M's, and above all else, she questions authority.

Hey, El, I love you. And most of all, I thank you.

↶ *Leslie Singer,* CUSTOM PUBLISHER

What is a friend?
A single soul in two bodies.

—ARISTOTLE

Black Clothes and *P*hone Calls

My friends are my counsel. I share with them in good times and bad. I look to them for guidance and support.

My friend Leslie and I talk on the phone almost every day. Sometimes, many times a day. We share things in ways we would never share with our spouses or our colleagues. We bitch, we moan, we laugh, we cry, and we finish each other's sentences. We share work, we share play. We talk about clothes, politics, the state of the world, and most importantly, how we feel about it all. I talk; she listens. She talks; I listen. We share our lives. And by the simple act of sharing, our lives become less isolated, less strange-feeling, more comfortable. The landscape of living may be a little weird, but Leslie and I are definitely in the same weird place together. What a relief!

We share the same profession. We're both creative. We go shopping together. Usually we fall in love with the same clothes. Sometimes we don't. But we share the passion of shopping together because we are together. We own some of the same things—special items—an outrageously expensive black coat, but it's so awesome; a black leather jacket; black pants. I wear these items and feel the bond between Leslie and me.

Of course, none of this magic is confined to Leslie and me. The men and women who talk in this chapter are just like me and my friend. We all bond through talking and through sharing our experiences and feelings—just like friends have done forever. We are all a part of the human community of friendships.

That's the beauty of true friendship; the beauty of a soul mate.

Friendships thrive on the good times, and the not so good, and sometimes it's the latter that show us how true friends can say things to us that no one else can. The best thing about friends is going through the same thing at the same time and finding out that they feel exactly the same way.

Surviving *M*otherhood . . . Together

T HAVE MET A NUMBER OF MY
FRIENDS IN FAIRLY STRANGE PLACES; one
example is the ladies' room at the Metropolitan Museum
of Art in New York City, where I worked. I was washing my
hands at the sink when I noticed a woman at the opposite
end of the room also washing her hands. She looked vaguely
familiar, but I couldn't quite place her. I could tell she was
also trying to figure out if she knew me, so I went over to
her and said, "I know I know you from somewhere, but I
don't know if I've seen you on TV, or if we went to college
together, or if you work at my dry cleaners." She laughed,
and as it turned out, I had seen her on TV (she had been
on a soap opera) and we had also gone to college together,
although we had been a year apart and hadn't really known

each other. She lived near the museum, and we found that we had little boys about the same age. We had a lot in common, from having gone to the same college to having briefly dated the same guy there (not at the same time). We became friends, and a few months later we both confessed that we were pregnant, and were due just a few weeks apart. The first time around I hadn't even known anyone with a baby, so it was wonderful to have someone to go through all the stages with.

> *It was wonderful to have someone to go through all the stages with.*
>
> —SOPHIE EVANS

When we were both around seven months pregnant, she called one day and said they were moving to the suburbs. I couldn't believe it. I knew that she and her husband had been thinking about moving, but I couldn't believe it had happened so quickly. We stayed in touch after she moved, but it wasn't the same as having her in the city.

One day when the babies were both about three months old I was miserable, exhausted, depressed—you name it. I felt like I couldn't cope with anything, and none of the parenting books or magazines answered any of the questions or addressed any of the issues that really concerned me, like, "What do you do when you feel like running away from home?"

That morning the phone rang, and it was her. Thank God, she was miserable, too. We started commiserating, and I immediately began to feel better. Then, at one point she said something that only another new parent could relate to. "Do you know what gets me through every day? Every day I think, 'I'll make it through today, and then one more day, and after many years, it'll all be over because I'll be dead.'"

There was a moment of shocked silence—on both our parts. We were both sort of stunned that she had actually said this—and then, suddenly, we both burst out laughing. It was a combination of enormous relief that one of us had vocalized how awful the first few months of having a baby can actually be, but also humor at the realization that what she had said was so ridiculous and over the top. Once she said that, I suddenly felt more cheerful, and knew that the "dark period" would in fact end, that things would get better (they did, of course), that we had both been rather melodramatic, and that it was lucky we had each other.

Everyone needs a friend that you can say things like that to.

Sophie Evans, EDUCATOR

ANYTIME CALL

*I*t's the friends you can call at 4 A.M. that matter.

—*Marlene Dietrich,*
ACTRESS

SOURCE: *Friends: A Treasury of Quotations*
(Philadelphia: Running Press, 1998)

Kathrine Switzer is a world-class runner. She won the 1974 New York City Marathon, broke the gender barrier at the 1967 Boston Marathon, and is an Emmy Award–winning TV commentator and author. A large part of the inspiration that helped her achieve her goals was provided by her good friend Ellie McGrath, a fellow marathon runner and a writer.

Inspired to Do It All

T MET ELLIE IN THE EARLY

'70s. I was a marathon runner—number three in the United States, number one in New York. Ellie was a very, very good runner, too. I'll never forget the first time I met her—it was at a meeting to discuss equal rights for women runners. I was a little in awe of her because she was a writer with *Time* magazine, and that was a very big deal to me. I had a full-time career, too, and I was crazy about Ellie because we were very much alike in an esoteric way—very career-minded, and under a lot pressure with our jobs, and yet totally committed to running well. She had these incredible deadlines, but she trained for the marathon, just like I did. I was very sympathetic.

We never thought that we "deserved" to train full

time—hell, *that* possibility didn't exist anyway, but more than that, we didn't want to be *just* runners. We wanted to be like the Greek philosopher-athletes: strong mind, strong body, strong everything. We shared a vision of what women could be. We intellectualized running a lot. It was all a *lot* more than running; in fact, I am sure part of our motivation for running was to display to the world and ourselves that we could do anything.

When I look back on it, we did. Now I think of those days and wonder how we kept our eyes open most of the time!

Eventually, I went into the business of actually organizing a global series of races called the Avon International Running Circuit, which was instrumental in creating the equality that we women runners were pushing for. To manage this career, I decided to stop being a competitive runner and just run for fitness. But Ellie was still racing hard, and I have wonderful photos of her running in the Avon series.

As time went on, Ellie put her own competitive running on the back burner, moved to San Francisco, and we each got married. Sometimes we didn't communicate for months, or even a year or two. I admired Ellie a lot because she really dug into things and just *did* it. When we didn't communicate for a while, it meant she had gone underground and written a book—just kept her head down and wrote. Boy, I admired that. It took me a long time to write a book, and when I did, it took a lot of glue to keep my butt in the chair. Ellie was a source of inspiration to me. I don't think I've ever told her that; I probably should. She eventually moved back to New York, started working for *Self* magazine, and had a baby.

> *I* was crazy about Ellie because we were very much alike in an esoteric way.
>
> —KATHRINE SWITZER

Every time I had an idea for an important article, I'd call Ellie. She was always fast on the case, too. She had her baby kind of late in her reproductive life, and it was soon after that, I think I was forty-four, when I experienced an early menopause. I called her immediately, since I thought there was an interesting investigative piece on whether there was a correlation between that and running, and she, more than anyone, would get it. She did, and *Self* did a big piece, a really pioneering piece, on the subject. Sometimes she worked from home when she had the baby, and it was always funny to be talking about menopause while hearing a baby yelling in the background. Once again, I admired her a lot; she could do difficult mental things while balancing a lot else.

When Avon came back to sponsoring women's running in the late '90s, I invited Ellie to the press conference. She was so excited. It marked a wonderful cycle in women's running. We'd fought hard for acceptance, we'd even channeled a lot of our careers in that direction, we'd succeeded, and now we were back in running and fitness for the best reason of all—because we loved it. When the Avon 10K race took place in New York, we ran together. We had run in this race together many times, but never side by side. It was wonderful. We talked the whole way about serious stuff—the big Life Balance. We pulled along a whole group of women who listened in on the conversation and then put their two cents in. The best part was when we veered across the road to slap hands with Ellie's little girl and husband, who were cheering for us.

Little did I know it then, but Ellie was just about to leave *Self* magazine to hunker down and write another book. I knew I'd probably not see her again for another six months! But the last thing she did at *Self* was to inspire the editor-in-chief to write her editor's letter about us running together after all these years, and the cycle of our lives.

We're still friends. We haven't had dinner in six months—but it doesn't matter. If I needed her, she would be immediately available.

Kathrine Switzer, RUNNER AND TV COMMENTATOR

Women *W*arriors

*K*ATHRINE HAS BEEN A HERO TO SO MANY WOMEN RUNNERS. I will never forget that famous picture of Jock Semple, the director of the Boston Marathon, trying to throw "K. Switzer" out of the race in 1967 because women were not allowed to run. Because of Kathrine and the other pioneers, I was allowed to put on a number and officially race in the 1976 New York Marathon.

As Kathrine has said, it wasn't just about running. Yes, we loved to race, but a lot of us were out to prove that women could do anything. Kathrine sometimes used to race in a tennis dress, her long hair tied back by a ribbon, to emphasize her femaleness. I followed her

lead and wore ribbons and earrings whenever I raced.
We may have privately viewed ourselves as women
warriors, but we had no desire to terrify others.

Running was very political in the 1970s, and Kathrine
was a master strategist. Once women were allowed to
enter marathons, the next step was to get a women's marathon included in the Olympics. Once again, Kathrine was a pathfinder. The International Olympic Committee

> *For us, the race was a celebration of fitness, friendship, and philosophy.*
>
> —ELLIE MCGRATH

initially claimed that there were not enough women
worldwide to include a marathon in the games. Kathrine
convinced Avon to sponsor women's marathons all over
the world. By 1984, the IOC agreed to include a women's
marathon and Joan Benoit won the gold medal.

When Kathrine and I reunited to run the Avon 10K
together, I felt joyful to still be running after all these
years beside such an inspirational friend. For us, the race
was a celebration of fitness, friendship, and philosophy—
of youth not completely lost and certainly not misspent.

Ellie McGrath, RUNNER AND WRITER

DELIGHTFUL

*T*here were equal measures of comfort and amusement in our communications; I think it is safe to say that we delighted in one another. She used to laugh at my stories until I wept, and I tried to take her sound advice to heart.

—*Jane Hamilton,* AUTHOR

SOURCE: *Friends: A Treasury of Quotations* (Philadelphia: Running Press, 1998)

Two world-class gymnasts from the 1992 U.S. Olympic medal-winning team, Shannon Miller and Kim Zmeskal, couldn't be more different on the outside, nor more similar inside. The media tried to make them rivals, but they became best friends instead.

Against
All *O*dds

*I*T'S DIFFICULT SOMETIMES TO MAKE AND KEEP FRIENDS WHO ARE OUTSIDE THE GYMNASTICS COMMUNITY— we're a pretty tight-knit family. We form these friendships from the time we're eight years old, though we're in different states and sometimes even different countries; we have really good friendships. Sometimes high school friends or college friends seem to be not quite as close because it's not what you're doing every day. We spend so much time in the gym.

I'm really close with a couple of gymnasts. It's really good for me to have gymnasts as close friends, and I think it's good for them too, because sometimes you feel like you're the only one who has to go through all these problems and then you talk to them and it's like they've been there, they've done that, or they're going through that right now.

You get to talk to each other and figure out how you're supposed to handle it, and together you go through it.

Kim Zmeskal is my best friend. She and I had seen each other in competitions for years, but we had different coaches and didn't really talk. Then in 1996 we were on tour together and haven't stopped talking since!

On the bus we would sit up front in the lounge area—there are two couches up front—listen to Garth Brooks and talk about our dates. We were the only two who listened to much country music. And we wouldn't go to bed. Instead we'd stay up listening to country and talk and talk and get a little bit sad. I remember that. It was nice having someone to go through this with.

> *The nicest thing about any friend is that they're there for you—you can always call them and talk to them and they're honest with you. That's Kim.*
>
> —SHANNON MILLER

When we were growing up and competing, before 1992, the media made us out to be rivals. It was funny because we didn't really know each other then and neither of us ever had that feeling of competition with each other. The competition for gymnastics is with the equipment. The point is to go out there and stay on the equipment! When we went on tour together in 1996 and really got to know each other, we laughed about it. It's really funny that the media made us out to be something we never were.

The nicest thing about any friend is that they're there for you—you can always call them and talk to them and they're honest with you. That's Kim. When I have a problem with any part of my life, I can go to my best friend, Kim, because she's not going to judge me and it's not going to be a big deal. Like all friends, she's just going to tell me what she thinks and try and help me out in any way she can. And often I'm lucky and Kim's been through it before.

୶ *Shannon Miller,* GYMNAST

Country Music,
All Night *L*ong

*W*E'VE SEEN EACH OTHER FOREVER. We had both been in the same region competing, but it was years before we got to become friends. The first time we really met was in 1990, when we both had progressed and were invited to compete in the American Cup. My coach hadn't flown in yet, so Shannon's coach, Steve Nunno, invited me to lunch. I knew from the start she was a nice sweet person; a little bit shy. I really liked her and felt connected to her. Even though we were different, we were the same. The media would explain our personalities in public as Shannon is the shy one and I'm the outgoing one. We really couldn't be more different, but really the same.

It's amazing, but years passed before we were really able to get to know each other. It was 1996 and we were both performing on the John Hancock tour and we just started talking and instantly connected. I found out that she's not as quiet as I thought she was.

We would stay on the tour bus all night, neither of us could sleep, and listen to country music and talk and talk and talk. We're really a lot alike. We both have the same feelings and the same fears. But it makes it easier to go through it with Shannon. She's a very intelligent woman. She brightens my day when I'm around her. Shannon's and my friendship is the best thing that happened on the tour. I'm so grateful that I got to know Shannon.

We don't get to see each other as much as we used

to, but we e-mail a lot. We just went out yesterday, driving around. We ditched our husbands—we both got married last year, both to guys named Chris—and we went driving. And it was great. We got lost, which was great because we got to spend more time together talking. It was so much fun. Shannon's really the only person who understands certain things because our lives are so much the same. It makes me so comfortable to talk to her. I miss seeing her more.

> *W*e're really a lot alike. We both have the same feelings and the same fears.
>
> —KIM ZMESKAL

You know the best thing is that we never had to pretend we were friends; we're just best friends.

Kim Zmeskal, GYMNAST

SAFTEY NET

Soul-friendships are the safety net of the heart.

—Susan Jeffers,
AUTHOR AND LECTURER

SOURCE: *Friends: A Treasury of Quotations*
(Philadelphia: Running Press, 1998)

When you're young and have a really good friend, it seems no miracle is impossible so long as it keeps you and your friend close and preserves the magical world you inhabit together. For Barbara and Kate, the miracles included flowers that could stop a construction crew and two improbably matching "with it" outfits.

*W*ildflowers to

Stop Bulldozers

I WAS SO YOUNG WHEN I MET BARBARA THAT I CAN'T REMEMBER NOT KNOWING HER. I was three when my family moved to a new town, to the little house at the foot of a steep hill where I grew up. It must have been right away that my mother encountered Barbara's mother and we two girls became friends. I know exactly how she looked then from pictures— a slender towhead, tall for her age, with a Dutch-boy haircut.

Barbara lived up the hill, at the end of a lane. My house was surrounded by other houses, and going to visit her seemed a little like going into the country. There was a large field on her lane, with a big hollow tree at the turn and several old, unused greenhouses which had been part of her father's business. Her father and his brothers had been florists, but Barbara's dad had come to fatherhood late in life and was already retired by the time we went to school. Her house sat back on a wooded property with a beautiful weeping cherry out front and several tall holly trees along the side. A path ran from her house into some woods, where we often played.

When we were seven or eight we heard the terrible news that the field had been sold to a developer, and we devised a plan to prevent any construction. From somewhere we got packs of wildflower seeds and sprinkled them all over the field, hoping that such a tangle would grow up that no bulldozers would be able to get through. It was a tragic day for us when the field was leveled for the eight new houses that rose soon after.

> *Every day when we walked home from school we decided whose house we would play at.*
>
> —KATE NORRIS

Every day when we walked home from school we decided whose house we would play at. We made up games, often based on books we had read. We talked about everything and we told each other everything. Barbara was a good writer and, over the years, she made up several songs with nonsense words that I still remember. One year, when we were about twelve, we decided to have a Christmas party for our friends at Barbara's house. We planned a treasure hunt and I made little stockings for each girl that would be filled with goodies and hidden around the house. One of us had the idea of making corsages of holly for everyone, and we cut sprigs from the trees outside. We had no concrete idea of how to put them together, and while we worked at them we also started to compose a poem (not about holly, for some reason, but about a rosebud), and before we knew it our first guest had arrived and nothing was set up. We had to chase our friend Meg from room to room while we hid the little stockings.

In seventh grade, after being teased in gym class about my hand-me-down clothes and lack of style, I asked my mother to take me shopping for a "with it" outfit. I ended up with a red bodysuit with a pattern of small white flowers and a pair of baby-blue bell-bottoms with white piping down the sides. Despite the fact that, looking back at it, this does not seem the most natural combination in the world, the next day, when I wore it to school, I found out from Barbara that she had recently bought the same outfit. We often ended up wearing it the same day. We took this as confirmation of what we knew already—that we were soul sisters.

Kate Norris, FREELANCE COPY EDITOR AND WRITER

WORDSMITHING

*I*t's rare to find someone you get on with so well. He was my best friend on the show for five years. George {Clooney} could finish my sentences for me.

—*Julianna Margulies,*
ACTRESS

SOURCE: Gary Warner, *Best Friends Forever*
(White Plains: Peter Pauper Press, 2000)

our friends are the most Accepting ever

*To know someone here or
there with whom you can
feel there is understanding in
spite of distances or thoughts
expressed. That can make
life a garden.*

—GOETHE

Finish Line Serenity

The Serenity Prayer asks for the courage to change what
can be changed, the serenity to accept what can't, and
the wisdom to know the difference. I think it could be
renamed the Friendship Prayer, because good friends
are really all about acceptance.

It is wonderful knowing that I can be myself (even if

the me of the moment is being foolish or mistaken) and my friends will still love and accept me. And it is just as wonderful to accept our friends as they are. We nudge each other to be our best selves, but in the end we accept. The truth is, the human flaws we all share often make our friends love us more.

My old running partner, Stephanie, used to run at a slower pace for my benefit. We used to race through Central Park. One particularly grueling race, Stephanie stayed behind and ran with me. At the finish line, I got a burst of energy and ran through ahead of her. I'll never forget how horrible I felt that I hadn't been as good a friend to her as she had to me. I apologized and Stephanie understood. She accepted me, my strengths and weaknesses, because I was her good friend. When we accept our friends, we create strong bonds that cannot be broken.

The people in this chapter show the deeply human side of their friends and friendships, proving once again that the more honest and open we are, the closer our relationships become. It is one of the sweetest ironies of life.

Malachy McCourt is the author of best-sellers A Monk Swimming *and* Singing My Him Song. As an actor, he became a beloved regular on TV. He shares the lesson that you often find friendship in places you're not taught to look. The most enduring friends can be a wife, like Malachy's Diana, or a brother, like Frank McCourt, the author of yet more best-sellers, like *Angela's Ashes*. And the most comforting conversation can be silence.

Singing His
Them ♪ong

RIENDSHIP ALWAYS HAS
BEEN VERY IMPORTANT TO ME FROM
CHILDHOOD. I think I've always had a very good
friend, and then we seem to drift apart. Often, you can
invest friends with virtues, almost the almighty powers
of God. Maturing is knowing they're not God and that
all friends, in big ways and little ways, will let you down.
Being able to survive that is the test of friendship.

I grew up in Limerick, where the traditional friendships
of boyhood were with the boys in your neighborhood, your
school. For a long time I didn't have many friends because
I was moving around a lot.

Then I married Diana. Before her, I never thought you
could also have your lover as a friend. I thought you had to

be so romantic, so perfect, that any kind of vulnerability had to be hidden. With friends, you don't really do that. You don't hide things. Your trust is one of the great things. So Diana turns out to be, as it happens, my best friend—my best female friend. And as it turns out, my brother Frank happens to be my best male friend.

They are both, in a sense, very nonjudgmental. They accept my weaknesses, my vulnerabilities as a human being, and they have taught me that a comment on a character defect is not a criticism. Rather, it is a friend's way of saying that it would do *you* a lot of good if you could correct something for yourself; it's not about *their* convenience.

> *M*aturing is knowing... that all friends, in big ways and little ways, will let you down. Being able to survive that is the test of friendship.
>
> —MALACHY MCCOURT

I used to be very defensive about things in that way and I'm not anymore. I now listen and say, "Ah." I was always looking out for criticism and someone looking to put me down, having had a lot of experience with that in my life. And so now I don't look for that. I now say, "Oh yeah, good idea, I'll try that. I should tie my shoelaces."

I'm always looking for the good in my friends and I'm so appreciative when I find it. When I get the phone call if I'm not feeling so hot; the congratulations when I do something good; people showing up at celebratory times, like a reading or the publication of a book. Or when a child is born or a grandchild—all of the celebrations of life and the sadnesses. It's people not being afraid.

One of the things with friends is that they're comfortable not having to say something. They don't have to be effusive. Like in times of sorrow or grief, people just showing up and taking your hand and giving you a hug. I appreciate that in men, too, because there's a certain thing that only in times of war or sports can men touch each other—so they're not considered queer. I can get a hug now from my male friends and it's okay. There's a certain characteristic in Irish people—men don't touch each other.

Gerard South is a good friend from childhood who I see when I go back to Ireland. I still consider him a good friend. We were in the scouts together. He's a very decent, wonderful human being. He used to make this neighing, horselike noise. He could do it without moving his lips. He could throw his voice. He would do it in the most sacred of circumstances, knowing it would collapse me and get me in trouble. He would do it in church, school, anywhere. And nobody would attribute it to him because his lips didn't move. A very decent guy.

He's a devoted man. His wife is severely affected by strokes and his son is retarded, and he looks after them. I still think of him as a kid and I can't imagine looking after people in that way. I admire him. I treasure his friendship. I don't talk to him that much, but whenever I go there I see him.

And then I have friends from a 12-step program. They are always there. There are about three guys I can talk to at length. They don't mind it at all if I moan and whine and complain and talk about approaching depression. So that's very important to me, to be able to do that.

Malachy McCourt, WRITER, ACTOR, RACONTEUR

Lisa had many acquain-tances, but none with whom she felt she could be completely herself. Because of the honesty of one woman, Lisa now has an inner circle of loved ones and confidantes.

$\mathcal{F}$riends

Don't Hide

$\mathcal{I}$ 'VE LIVED JUST OVER FOUR
DECADES AND I'VE HAD A FEW BEST
FRIENDS IN MY LIFE. But whenever I think back,
I always know that no friend has done more for me than
Deirdre, the friend who taught me how friendship works.

The first best friend I remember was Lilly, who had
long red hair; we would try to dress up her baby sister
Patsy each afternoon after our kindergarten class. Lilly's
mother always had chocolate chip cookies in the cookie jar,
which I think may have been one of the underlying reasons
for our year-long friendship. Lilly and Patsy moved away
the summer before first grade. In third grade, I met Amy,
and we immediately hit it off. Amy and I composed poetry
together at her kitchen table and made plans to become a

writing team after we graduated. I wish I knew what has become of Amy; she and her mother moved away during our fourth grade year, following her father's unexpected death. I remember clearly how helpless I felt when Amy would break into tears in the weeks following her father's wreck, and how I longed to trade places with her to take some of the pain.

Several friendships through my life have been based on a mutual love of the arts. In high school, rather than memorize a scene from a play to perform, Martha Anne and I would make up a fictitious playwright, fib to Miss Williams about how long we'd been practicing our lines, and then ad lib ten minutes of high drama on the spot. Usually, the scenes were based loosely on whatever was going on at the moment. Thus, we did failed love stories, based on Martha's breakup with her boyfriend; parent-child fights, based on the ongoing problems between my mother and me; and comedy pulled straight from Martha's driving lessons.

Because of rough times at home, it was often difficult for me to open up my life to my friends. I didn't want them on the inside. I didn't even want me on the inside of my life, much less anyone else. I knew how to steer every conversation back to the person in front of me, deftly avoiding revealing too much about myself.

In fact, I often felt that if I did reveal myself, it would push people away from me. This talent has served me professionally and personally because others enjoy the interest I show in them; unfortunately, it also ended up sabotaging my friendships.

I remember well when Deirdre gently let me know that, in spite of sharing an apartment through college and through our first jobs, she felt I was a stranger. I had just taken a new job in a new city. I had no connections, no history, no friendships. A clean slate, I thought. It rapidly felt more like an empty slate. Although it was easy to forge friendships through the churn and burn of work, it was difficult to achieve any real depth.

> *I had a whole new understanding of friendship. In fact, it was selfish not to talk about myself. If I refused to show my weaknesses, they couldn't offer their strengths.*
>
> —LISA WALTERS

Although I could pull information from the women with whom I worked about their workdays, their boyfriends, and their lives, I felt more like a reporter than a friend. I longed for someone with whom I could have a heart-to-heart talk, someone with whom I could

share how insecure I felt about work, someone I could
tell about the attractive man who lived next door.
Finally, I picked up the phone and called Deirdre.

"It's so great to hear from you," she said. "How's it
going?"

I immediately turned the question around, with
"No, you first! Tell me what's new."

She obliged, and spent the next several minutes giving
me an update. When she was finished, I felt renewed. I
felt like I was part of someone else's life again. She pressed
again to get me to open up, and I closed the conversation, unable to speak about myself. I gave her general
answers, and assured her I was fine. We said good-bye,
and I went to bed happier than I had been for weeks.

Within a few days of our conversation, the card that
changed my life arrived. It was from Deirdre, and was brief
and to the point. The sentence that stood out was this:
"It hurts my feelings when you refuse to let me be a
friend."

In that instant, Deirdre changed my perspective
and my life. I had always thought my demonstration of
interest in others was why they liked me. It was uncom-
fortable to open up, and it felt selfish to talk about myself.
Now I had a whole new understanding of friendship.
In fact, it was selfish *not* to talk about myself. It kept

my friends from giving so much to me, like advice and comfort. Because if I refused to show my weaknesses, they couldn't offer their strengths.

I called Deirdre the night I got the card. I told her what I had learned, I thanked her, and then I apologized for not letting her get closer to me. I cried that night, the first time I had ever cried in earshot of someone outside of my own family. Hours later, we ended the phone call in laughter, with Deirdre promising to help me break my own silence by actually interviewing me. And she did. In the conversations we had over the next four weeks, Deirdre learned more about me than she had known in five years of living together.

Deirdre will always be my best friend, and because of her, I now have a close circle of friends with whom I share my life. Deirdre opened up a whole world for me, a world that would be awfully lonely without her.

    Lisa Walters, WEB PRODUCER

I'M OKAY

You know what's good? To have somebody ground you and say "Wait, it's okay."

—*Jennifer Aniston,*
ACTRESS

SOURCE: Gary Warner, *Best Friends Forever*
(White Plains: Peter Pauper Press, 2000)

Sometimes you miss an opportunity to tell your friends how you really feel, but if you're lucky, like Vincent, you get the chance again.

Second *C*hances

*J*ASON HAD MOVED THREE
YEARS AGO. We were eleven when he left for Texas.
Jason, Gary, and I were inseparable before that day. In winter
we played football in the snowy field next to Gary's house.
Spring saw us swinging baseball bats and lying in the cool
green grass under a lemon yellow sun. Each summer day
we'd ride our bikes to the Hobby Shop to buy baseball
cards and eat at Pizza Village. There was nothing better
than that pizza and an ice cold Pepsi on a sweltering day.
But Jason had moved—three became two.

Jason made a yearly pilgrimage from Texas to New
Jersey. His grandmother still lived in Jersey. Otherwise we
spoke every so often on the phone.

We turned fourteen. It was my turn. My family was

moving and not under the best of circumstances. At the time I never thought I'd miss that white house. I'd figured all the bad would be left behind there. I was glad to be leaving it. I didn't know it would follow us.

Gary helped me finish packing. The car was ready. Gary and I stood in front of the garage like we had so many times. I was not sad. The ramifications of the move were still not real. Gary stared at me. His eyes filled with pain and anger as if I had just killed his dog. There were tears in his eyes. I'd like to say that I grabbed him and hugged him tight and told him we would still be as close as ever. I'd like to say that. Instead I slapped his hand as I would have if I was going to see him the next day to play hoops down at Lloyd Road or wait for the Red Bank Catholic girls to get off the bus on my corner. Gary jumped on his bike. Fourteen is the last year boys ride bikes in the suburbs. He rode down the hill to go home. My mother pulled the car out of the driveway and a chapter in my life concluded.

Gary and I spoke often on the telephone. I was an outsider in Toms River at first. It was a tough place to make new friends, especially in a town where the financial prosperity of your family determined your social status. Like I said, we hadn't left Matawan for the better. Eventually I made good friends. Gary made new ones.

We spoke less on the phone. I went to college. He did not. Gary came to visit me at school. We made time to see each other, but no longer was it in the field next to his house (his family sold the land to developers). But there was still a bond that neither of us would break. We saw each other in bars or birthday dinners or holiday parties.

One night last year Gary asked me to be an usher at his wedding. His brother was the best man. I told him the story about the day I moved from Matawan and how much it had hurt me to leave. I told him that I was sorry I did not hug him and say I understood that he was mad and upset as well because he went through all of it with me. I told him that I knew he must have felt betrayed as both his best friends left him. We hugged and told each other that we loved one another.

> We hugged and told each other that we loved one another.
>
> —VINCENT FALIVENE

The day of his wedding I stood in a tight-fitting tuxedo. As he exchanged vows with the woman he chose to spend his life with, I cried. A hand touched my shoulder and asked me if I was okay. I turned to the usher standing next to me and told Jason that I would be fine.

Vincent Falivene, WRITER

51

Ellen and Jane had an immediate connection, despite an eleven-year age difference. Yet it took years and hard work for the relationship to become one of equals. What allowed their friendship to evolve was a deep-rooted trust that enabled them to accept each other at every stage.

My Youngest,
Oldest *friend*

Y FRIEND JANE IS MY OLDEST FRIEND. She's actually my youngest oldest friend. I met her when I was her sixth-grade math teacher. She was eleven and I was twenty-two. It was my first teaching job. I was a junior high school math teacher and she was in my homeroom and my math class.

Although she was a very precocious kid and very popular in her class, she always felt a little out of place. So it was great that we made an immediate connection. I was like an older sister to her. I never knew or anticipated that she was someone I was going to know for my entire life.

We really got to know each other when Jane was elected president of her seventh-grade class and I was the student council adviser. She used to stay after school and come to my room to help out. When it was time to go home, Jane would walk me to my car and I'd drive her home. Jane would talk and we'd have these incredibly intimate conversations about her life and the struggles she was having. Junior high school is a hard age of transition.

Over time I got to know her family. I played tennis with her mother and got to know her older sister and her brother. The friendship between Jane and me just grew and grew. Over the years, it's gone through incredible phases—me being like an older sister, me being a role model, then, in some ways being someone she resented, and then finally, a peaceful place of accepting and loving each other as peers.

> *And at every stage we accepted each other, which is how we got so close.*
>
> —ELLEN BIALO

I think she worked out with me some of the issues she had with her mother. The first few times Jane got angry with me were a big deal. But it enabled us to get closer. And now she's my closest friend. She's an incredibly introspective, wonderful woman who gives so much to me. We're able to say anything to each other—we totally accept each other.

I'm now fifty-three and she's forty-two. I've known her for thirty-one years. It's amazing and really rewarding to watch someone grow up, to see somebody through all those life stages, and to have that kind of history with a person. We're so close because our relationship grew into a relationship where we truly became peers and we really know one another. We have an incredibly strong foundation.

Our relationship has endured all these years because as she grew, I grew, too. And at every stage we accepted each other, which is how we got so close. We facilitated each other's growth. Jane was very willing to take risks, say things, and give me feedback, not just on our friendship, but also about things I was doing in life. And I did the same with her.

We always had this trust where we could say anything and know the other person was not going to go away. We could get angry and know we were not going to leave each other, because we so accepted each other. I'm sure we'll be old together. It's that type of friendship.

Ellen Bialo, PRESIDENT OF INTERACTIVE
EDUCATIONAL SYSTEMS DESIGN

INSPIRATION

*T*he glory of friendship is not the outstretched hand, nor the kindly smile, nor the joy of companionship; it is the spirited inspiration that comes to one when he discovers that someone else believes in him and is willing to trust him with his friendship.

—Ralph Waldo Emmerson,
POET

Real best friends can be loving, infuriating, wonderful, and frustrating—but that's part of what makes them who they are. Susan found this out with her free-spirited friend Peggy, who ended up in her life in a way Susan could never have predicted.

Cupid for
a *friend*

I WAS WORKING AT A SCHOOL IN NEW YORK and I went out a couple of times with a guy I met there. I was living with my son and, when we moved into our own apartment, the guy came over a couple of times and brought his sister, Peggy, and her husband. I had no furniture—just milk crates. They would come over and we would play games; we all got along really well.

One day Peggy called me up on her own and asked if she could come over with her husband, Joseph. She started coming over more often with him. We all liked to sing—we had contests. We had decided that we were going to be famous singers.

One time we went looking for a singing teacher who was giving lessons to Peggy's brother. We knew the street, but not the address. We spent two hours roaming around, looking for it. Peggy was wearing this white outfit and, as we got out of a cab, I noticed that her skirt was covered with blood. I took her to the hospital and stayed with her for three hours. It turned out she had had a miscarriage. Joseph was really appreciative that I had stayed with her and we became even closer.

We did all sorts of crazy stuff. We used to call up radio stations and pretend we were the managers of a band. We went to the station at 8 A.M. in full makeup. She used to take me to interviews with her so I could translate—she didn't speak much English. One time she taught at a modeling school, and I went with her. Peggy would talk to the Spanish girls, and I would "translate" for the ones who spoke English. We did everything together. When she opened an office, we looked at all the furniture and stuff together. I worked with her for a while, but it got to be too much. I quit and our friendship got better again.

Then Peggy separated from Joseph and moved to

> *W*e did all sorts of crazy stuff. We used to call up radio stations and pretend we were the managers of a band.
>
> —SUSAN SANCHEZ

Puerto Rico. I got to know her better when she moved away. When she was here, we fought a lot. After she moved, I could tell her things I couldn't before. At one point, I pointed out that her current boyfriend was away for all the "gift-giving" holidays. She lost a few boyfriends along the way. Then she moved to Miami where some of her family lived. My cousin also lived in Florida; he had gotten divorced. Peggy called one day when I was on the phone with him. I told Charles, my cousin, that he and Peggy might get together. I went back to Peggy, and told her, "Don't get romantic with him, but he's a really nice guy."

> *We did everything together. When she opened an office we looked at all the furniture and stuff together.*
>
> —SUSAN SANCHEZ

Peggy put him off at first—she said he sounded fat over the phone. When they had their first date, I called when he got to her house. He thought Peggy was beautiful. I kept calling back the entire night—I basically went on the date with them on my cell phone. Good thing he worked for a phone company so I didn't have to pay for it. After the date I got to hear both sides of the story. He really liked her, and she thought he was a total gentleman. She said he was "normal."

I was with them through the whole courtship on the cell phone.

Six months later they got married.

I didn't end up going to the wedding, and I felt really terrible. I called during the reception and Peggy said she was sending me a letter. I was afraid to get it, but it was incredibly nice. I thought she would have said all sorts of stuff about why I hadn't been there, but she didn't. It wasn't what I expected. I told her I would write her back, even if it took years to write it. There's no one else like her.

I'm so glad she picked me to be her best friend, and not someone else.

Susan Sanchez, BOOKSTORE ASSISTANT MANAGER

SELF-EXAMINATION

I can trust my friends...
These people force me
to examine myself,
encourage me to grow.

—*Cher,* ACTRESS

SOURCE: Gary Warner, *Best Friends Forever*
(White Plains: Peter Pauper Press, 2000)

our friends are the most f*un ever*

Laughter is not at all a bad beginning for a friendship, and it is by far the best ending for one.

—OSCAR WILDE

Dead-End Streets and Silly Fashions

Two against the world is a lot better odds than one. And when friends understand that they're together to make it fun, even the rough times get smooth and the laughter drowns out the screechy noises made by bad bosses and even bad marriages.

Fun is the best defense against our less-than-perfect world. And the first step toward making it more perfect. Two friends laughing together at life's most minor mishaps strengthens the bonds of their friendship.

Having fun together is the first way we make friends. My first best friend was Paula. She was the seventh child of my neighbors. We lived on a dead-end street and Paula and I would run up and down the street laughing—just the two of us. No one else knew what we were laughing at, sometimes not even us; but we loved that it was just between us.

As I grew older the fun times remained just as important. Even as my friendships changed and grew, every close friend shared the gift of a sense of humor and laughter with me.

Our sense of humor changes. My friend Leslie and I laugh all the time; but now we laugh about world affairs, the silly fashions we can no longer wear, the client who acts just like a client, or the boss who just won't listen. We share the same perspective on life, which means we are able to laugh together.

Whoever said laughter is the best medicine was right—it's also the glue that holds friendships together. To laugh together at life's ridiculous turn of events makes those events bearable. To laugh at the funny things in life makes life wonderful. The real gift is having a friend to share my laughter with. To all the friends who share their fun in this chapter, thanks for the laughs.

Great friends share attitude.
They take on the world together
before they're out of the ninth
grade. They laugh in the face
of adversity. They even go to
see kinky rock dramas featuring
men in women's underwear.
And they have so much fun . . .

$\mathcal{G}$irls in Black

$\mathcal{S}$TANDING ON THE CORNER OF 70TH AND BROADWAY IN OUR BLACK LIPSTICK AND FISHNET TIGHTS, we felt surges of excitement. We were on our way to see *The Rocky Horror Show* live on Broadway. When we reached Circle in the Square Theatre, we felt a little bit strange; approximately 8 percent of the people there were dressed like we were. But, not to worry, by the time the show started much of the audience looked similar to us. My friend was glowing, as much as she could through white makeup, and very close to shaking from the antici(say it!)pation.

Sitting in the maroon plush seat next to her during the show, shouting out audience participation (she getting into it much more than me), I was so happy. It was the first time I had brought one of my friends with me to see my dad in New York and she was the perfect one— always enthusiastic, taking pictures everywhere, and being an all-around fun person.

When the show was over we couldn't believe it had actually happened. The night before we had been in the Village having dinner and wandering around in the rain, looking in the stores and vendor carts. At The Sock Man, we found more items to add to our Rocky Horror outfits, including two black feather boas and, much to my friend's delight, a black vinyl skirt. The morning of the show we thoroughly scared a sweet, elderly drugstore cashier by buying a large supply of black makeup, hair dye, and a little extra black nail polish (just in case). Later that night, while putting (actually it was more like caking) it all on, we were having so much fun that it didn't matter where we were or what we were doing. It was just simply fun to be with a friend.

> *We* thoroughly scared a sweet, elderly cashier by buying a large supply of black makeup.
>
> —AMY CHEYFITZ

Amy Cheyfitz, AGE FIFTEEN, PAM'S FRIEND

It's a big world and some-times it can get a little dicey, so it's a lot more fun to navigate with a buddy. Pegi and Jessie have been friends since college and now finish each other's sentences, when either can get a word in between the laughter. Pegi and Jessie have been through it all together, but because they're friends, they're still laughing.

*L*aughter Is the
Best Medicine

WE INVENTED FUN.
I remember when we were twenty-three, riding in a convertible together, a Karmen Ghia, driving into the sunlight, nothing but friendship on our minds, and it was cold and the top was down and we were singing at the top of our lungs with the heat on, laughing. Life is short. Why not?

We met when we were eighteen years old and have been friends ever since. We lived together in a place we called the Kennel, a hot-water flat where we raised dust kittens! (We had heard of a cold-water flat, but this one only had hot water!) We lived with this great guy, Bill, who is still a great friend of ours. You could only wash one dish at a time because there was no cold water except in the toilet. And you had to run half of your bath the night before, so there would be cold water in the tub to make a warm bath in the morning. We had the worst possible jobs in New York. But we had a blast.

We just loved each other. There's no two ways about it. We'd been in college together, but we weren't really, really good friends in college. It was when we moved in together after college that we had the most fun. Lots of laughs. Jessie was married at the time, getting unmarried, and her husband came to the apartment and said, "You would rather live with Pegi Goodman than me?" And Jessie said, "Yes."

The first year that we lived together sealed it. We had publishing jobs in New York. In the spring, we quit our jobs and ended up living up at Jesse's parents' house with a cousin and a friend of hers. They were totally straight and had come to New York to start their careers—lawyers or something. And Jessie and I would be up all night crocheting handbags, watching TV, and drinking beer. In the morning, they'd be in their dresses and heels off to work and we'd be just rubbing our eyes.

We sold the handbags at craft fairs. Today, we can't go to a craft fair without breaking out in a sweat. We had no money to pay the Con Ed bill and people would pick up our bags and say "Oh, I could do that." *Great.* But the neatest part is a month ago I called Pegi and said, "They're selling our bags at the Gap." Twenty years later. Ours were nicer. They were beautiful. I wish I still had some.

We always worked together. We never fought about work. We were at *The Village Voice* and *Rolling Stone*; we were at Golden Books when it was going bankrupt. If we could get along at Golden Books in those days, we could get along anywhere. We would run out at lunch and say to each other, "Okay, take a deep breath." It was crazy. Trying to figure out the schedules at Golden was impossible. We went to lunch with this big stack of schedules and tried to make sense of it and we just started laughing. We laughed and laughed. Laughing, that's our job.

The other amazing thing is that both our mothers died on the same day. Not the same year, but the same day. And Jessie and I are born on the same day—except she's older. It's the 19th—same year, different months. And Sam, my son, is born on the 19th. We have a thing with 19.

We had our hard times, too, but we always came

> *W*e had eleven dollars and Jessie wanted to get in the car and go cross country.
>
> —PEGI GOODMAN

through. We had one huge fight and that's it. We got over it right away. We had eleven dollars and Jesse wanted to get in the car and go cross country. I went home to my parents. Jesse got really mad at me because I wouldn't go with her. We didn't talk for about a few months. But then Jesse wanted to come back to New York, so she found a place and I got a job at *The Village Voice* and Jessie at Dell. We lived together. Forget the jobs. We had so much fun.

That's what friendship is about. The passion. When you love somebody, you eventually do have to quarrel with them because things will come to a head. You care. Even when we were both living on the edge, we kept it together in terms of our friendship. It's quite remarkable. If we'd been of the opposite sex, we'd be married.

Pegi Goodman, DESIGN DIRECTOR
Jessie Woeltz, EDITOR

At six, friendship isn't an abstract idea or a theory, it's pretty concrete. It's about wiggling noses, building with Legos, laughing like crazy, and doing other fun stuff together. It's also about not fighting. Come to think of it, every fun thing we learned about friendship, we learned by first grade. So it's good to know that Andrew already realizes the value of a real friend.

Feeding Babbit
the *Rabbit*

*T*HE BEST FRIEND I HAVE
EVER HAD IS ADAM. Adam is in my class and he has
brown hair and he lives six houses down from our house.
He is funny and knows a lot of knock-knock jokes, even
more than my mom. He teaches them to me, and then I
tell them to my family at dinner. I think we met this year,
since we just moved to San Francisco and he didn't live in
Dallas, which is where we used to live. We don't look anything alike, because I have blond hair and I'm taller. Adam
is wider than me, but we still wear each other's T-shirts.

When I got to take care of Babbitt the Rabbit during
Christmas break at my school, Adam came over and we
would feed Babbitt together. Babbitt likes me more, but he
and Adam get along just fine. Babbitt ate from our hands,
and then Adam and I tried to copy his pink nose wiggling.

Adam can do it better than I can. I can't make my nose move without moving my mouth a lot, but it makes Adam laugh every time I try.

Somehow, even though we don't always let others have a turn on Nintendo, Adam and I never fight over it. When I want to take a turn, it's okay with him, and when he's ready to take a turn, it's okay with me. I think that's one of the reasons that we are best friends. It was the same with Babbitt.

> *I can't make my nose move without moving my mouth a lot, but it makes Adam laugh every time I try.*
>
> —ANDREW LEWIS

I like to think about the different ways we can make starships with the Legos, and I think about how the pieces should fit together. Adam doesn't like that part so much, but he likes to build the ships. Mom says that we make quite a team. If I decide not to be a bus driver, maybe when we grow up, we'll open up a store together. Maybe not, since it's a long way off. It would be fun, though.

Andrew Lewis, AGE SIX

HAPPY DANCING

*J*ust thinking about a friend makes you want to do a happy dance, because a friend is someone who loves you in spite of your faults.

—*Charles Schulz,*
CARTOONIST

SOURCE: *Friends: A Treasury of Quotations*
(Philadelphia: Running Press, 1998)

Accepting one another without reservation is part of the magic about friendship. When behavior that ought to drive you crazy makes you laugh instead, then you know you've found a true friend.

Never Abandon *Y*our Bird

*L*IFE WITH SUSAN IS ALWAYS AN ADVENTURE. The trip to my hairdresser's is a perfect example.

I was doing her a favor, but the truth is I gave her a ride to assuage my own guilt, too—if my husband knew I was driving 250 miles just to get my hair cut, he'd never let me forget it.

I pick her up and discover it's not going to be just us in the car. Of course not. There's Lola, her pampered if sweet-tempered poodle, and the canaries. The canaries?

Apparently, Susan has recently acquired two American Singers, both Hartz canaries, but one of them very "rare." The rare one looks more plain to me than the other—more whitish than yellow, with a colorless tail, compared to the other's opalescent green wings. But the more colorful one, she says, is a marvelous singer. "If he were human," she gushes, "Bird-Guy would be a Pavarotti!"

My hairdresser, Marie, lives in suburban New Jersey. Susan stays in the car with her menagerie. But about halfway through my haircut, the doorbell of the salon rings. It's a teenage boy telling us Susan has borrowed his ladder and he has to go but please return it to him. Ladder? I cringe.

Next door to my hairdresser's, on a ladder, Susan is trying to coax one of her canaries back into her hand. It's Bird-Guy. His cage sits on the ladder's platform, with its door open and a wilted piece of lettuce sticking out of it. How did Bird-Guy wind up a free bird? Susan says she brought the cages outside because the birds "needed fresh air" and she thought Bird-Guy was choking. So she opened the door to reach in to help and whoof, Bird-Guy was out in a flash.

A few people have gathered on the edge of the neighbor's lawn. "Hey, you oughtta use a butterfly net!" one of them, an older man, calls out. But neither he nor any of the others has such a net. "How about usin' a stick?" somebody else yells. It's a helpful crowd.

I tell Susan I'll be back in a minute—I need to finish getting my hair done.

"It looks cute," she says sweetly. "Is she going to blow-dry it?"

Inside, Marie asks me if Susan is always like this. Like what? I remember the time Susan carried a two-by-four to the movies with us. She had picked it up along the walk to the cinema, thinking it would be terrific for her loft. The ticket booth clerk would not let us in.

We have been through jobs, boyfriends, a thousand different homes and projects, victories and defeats. I just can't leave her here in New Jersey on top of a ladder.

—LISA CHAMPEAU

When I return outside, Susan looks tired but still determined. Most of the neighbors have gone now. I take a deep breath and try to help.

"Here, Bird-Guy!" I whisper to myself. We try different strategies for two hours, before I tell Susan it all appears useless. But she refuses to go. "I'm staying," she says, not looking at me. "Just leave my bags (and Lola and the other bird) on the sidewalk. I'll call Ed to pick me up." Ed is her fiancé.

Susan and I go on debating for five more minutes, until I join her in her hunt again. She is, after all, my friend. We have known each other forever—since grad school. We have been through jobs, boyfriends, a thousand different homes and projects, victories and defeats. She introduced me to my husband. I just can't leave her here in New Jersey on top of a ladder. A borrowed ladder at that.

But I don't know who I'm more bewildered by—Susan or Bird-Guy.

Then, suddenly, finally, it happens. A miracle. Bird-Guy flies over to Susan, pokes at the lettuce and just walks into the cage. Boom. Susan shuts the door.

It's been a little under three hours.

About halfway through the Lincoln Tunnel, I start laughing. Then Susan starts laughing, too.

"I can't believe that bird flew back into captivity!" I shout. "I can't believe it!"

"Me either!" Susan says. And she's telling the truth. She was never sure we would be successful. She just didn't want to go, to be the one to abandon the other. I guess I feel the same way about her.

I really do have to find a local hairdresser, though.

∂ *Lisa Champeau*, JOURNALIST

*Teenagers need friends
the way orchids need water,*
but it's amazing we ever make
friends in our teens given the
awkwardness of the age. The
great thing about friendship is
that it has the power to over-
come the scariness of the new,
the awkwardness of the moment,
and all the other fears and
embarrassments of life and turn
them into something fun.

Dog Day
*A*fternoon

*W*HEN I WAS ELEVEN, WE
MOVED TO A NEW NEIGHBORHOOD WHERE
I had no friends. My brother had a friend who lived around
the corner; the friend had a sister, Samantha. One day
when my brother went to play with his friend, I very
offhandedly told him that if Samantha had nothing better
to do, she could come over. (I didn't want to appear too
enthusiastic for fear of rejection!) They were a somewhat
exotic family: half South African, half English, exceptionally
good looking, and, I assumed, *very* popular.

When Samantha appeared at the door, I was quite
amazed. It was a warm summer day, so we decided to be
very grown up and have tea in the garden with my dog,
Taffy, sitting calmly at my feet. Then, quite suddenly, something came over the dog and he became amorous with
Samantha's leg. Both of us were at the age when everything

is embarrassing, and we did our best to ignore Taffy, thinking that maybe he would stop. He did not. After close to half an hour of this, Samantha made an excuse to leave. I thought that would be the last time I saw her.

She called several days later and asked me to come play at her house. She and I became best friends. Over the next twenty years, our lives followed much the same course, although we didn't see each other very often. We both became actresses, we both unbecame actresses, we both had children, and she is my son's godmother. She is the friend that I can call even if we haven't spoken in six months and pick up just where we left off.

I have no doubt that she would always be there for me. She has taught me that proximity isn't the most important element to a friendship, that love and respect are what it takes. I am very fortunate that she had the strength of character to see beyond Taffy's advances.

> *S*he has taught me that proximity isn't the most important element to a friendship.
>
> —BERKELY ARRANTS

Berkely Arrants, FINANCIAL PLANNER

HA HA HA HA

*A*nd when we look at each other, our arms gummy from an orange Popsicle we split, we could be sisters, right? We could be you and me waiting for our teeth to fall and money. You laughing something into my ear that tickles, and me going Ha Ha Ha Ha.

—*Sandra Cisneros,* WRITER

SOURCE: Sandra Cisneros, *Woman Hollering Creek* (New York: Random House, 1991)

our friends
are the best *G*ift ever

We get by with a little help from our friends.

—JOHN LENNON AND PAUL MCCARTNEY

A Tale of
Two Scarves

Our friends give us so much, and then they give us more. My friends would do anything for me and me for them. That's what makes the bond so deep, so comforting, such a gift.

My friend Zanne listens to me incessantly, and then she listens more. When life is difficult, she knows I need to talk. That's how I work things out. So she gives me her ear, her time. She listens. She puts me back together. We meet in Starbucks. We drink lattes. I do most of the talking. When my first husband and I split up and I was going through one of the most difficult periods of my life, Zanne met me daily and listened. When that wasn't enough, she listened on the phone. The time of day or night never matters. We talk and life becomes hopeful again.

Our friends would give us the shirts off their backs—literally. My friend Leslie and I love scarves. She had given me a beautiful black velvet scarf with a white satin backing. I wore it every day in the fall and winter. I actually longed for cooler weather so I could wear it. One windy day I was walking down Broadway with my stepdaughter and the scarf disappeared. We searched and searched until we were frozen, but never found the scarf. When I told Leslie, without missing a beat, she gave me the solid black velvet scarf from around her neck. Whenever I wear it, I think of how giving Leslie is. She knew I gained comfort and joy from my scarf.

The giving need not be big or noticeable. It just needs to be a gift, freely given, with no thought to what might come in return.

The people in this chapter give to their friends. They give time, love, money, rides to the airport—and even scarves. But the real gift that always comes from friends, no matter what they are giving at the moment, is the gift of friendship.

The beauty of warm, giving people. The beauty of friends.

For Laurin Sydney, the cohost of *C.N.N's* Showbiz Today, it's the friend she speaks with the least whom she calls her best friend. They would do anything for each other, real or imagined, even splitting a favorite outfit.

The Gift of
the *M*agi

*I*T'S HARD TO PICK ONE BEST FRIEND, but when I think about it, one friend comes to mind—Norma. I speak with her the least. With lots of my friends, I know what they're having for dinner, I know what they're doing every day; not Norma. I just don't talk to her that often. But if I picked up the phone and called her and said, "Meet me in Istanbul in twenty minutes. Go to this lake that I don't know the name of, walk ten feet, go right, get naked, and yell," she would go without hesitation, without asking any questions.

We have this amazing, amazing relationship. This amazing bond is based on being like family. We're bound together spiritually. Her dad and my mom were very sick at the same time. An hour after my mom died, Norma called to tell me her dad had died. We couldn't be physically together, but we *were* together.

I can go a month without talking to Norma and we're still as close as ever. We talk about the real issues in our lives—the real stuff. We go straight to the gut. It's more than girl talk; it's soul talk.

We met about fifteen years ago in New York. We both came to New York to start our careers. We had no money. We went shopping and went into this store where we fell in love with a two-piece outfit. It was really different. The top was like a down vest, before down vests, and it was striped. It was cool. And of course there was only one left, which neither of us could afford. So, we reluctantly left. Later, I snuck back into the store and bought Norma one of the pieces. Later that night, when I gave it to her, she had done the same thing and bought me the other piece. It's the gift of the magi. It's true friendship.

> *W*e go straight to the gut. It's more than girl talk; it's soul talk.
>
> —LAURIN SYDNEY

Laurin Sydney, CNN ENTERTAINMENT REPORTER AND ANCHOR

A WEB OF FRIENDSHIP

*W*hy did you do all this for me?" he asked. "I don't deserve it. I've never done anything for you." "You've been my friend," replied Charlotte. "That in itself is a tremendous thing."

—*E. B. White*, AUTHOR

The Supper Club is one of those rare and wonderful meetings of minds that you thought you'd only encounter in a novel—a group of friends whose supportive, no-nonsense talk proved that an encouraging word (and a kick in the ass) can make all the difference. Meeting monthly, these six women really help each other to live their dreams. If you ever questioned the power of friendships, Elizabeth Cogswell Baskin's Supper Club of six women will change your mind.

The Power of
the ʃupper Club

*T*HAVE SIX BEST FRIENDS AND
WE ALL HAVE DINNER TOGETHER ONCE A
MONTH. We call it the Supper Club, and it is an amazing
group of women. It's tricky scheduling our dinners, because
everybody's so busy, but it's a huge priority for all of us
and we just make it work.

The group started after I had this awful birthday revela-
tion. It was a few years after I'd started my ad agency.
Because it was a start-up, it was all-consuming. For a long
time, all I did was work, sleep, and spend a very little bit of
time with my husband. That's it. I would do things like find
a stack of Father's Day cards sitting on my desk about a month
after Father's Day. I'd bought them, I'd even addressed them,
but I had been so crazy busy that I'd never mailed them.

On my birthday I came home early from work, thinking, "Well, I'll need a little extra time before dinner to open all my birthday cards and I'm sure I'll have a bunch of phone calls." Well, nobody called me and I only had one card and it was from my dentist. I even had to call my own mother to remind her it was my birthday. I realized then that I was losing touch with my family and friends in a really important way. I decided I had to build in time for the people I love, the same way I built in time for my business.

> *It's this incredible voodoo of these women that makes it happen.*
>
> —ELIZABETH COGSWELL BASKIN

Coincidentally, I had a close friend who was wanting to make some new friends and I kept telling her I would start her a book club. So I called up six of the coolest women I knew to start this book club, and they all seemed sort of lukewarm on it. Then my cousin, who never minces words, said, "Oh, nobody wants to read a bunch of books. Let's just eat and drink and call it a Supper Club." And everyone loved that. So that's how it all started.

It is an incredibly powerful group of friends. We accelerate each other's lives. In fact, one of the women who was at our first few suppers told us she hated her job, something in computers, and what she really wanted to do was work for Sotheby's. Well, she couldn't make the next get-together because she'd moved to Chicago for a new job—at Sotheby's!

One dinner, I announced that my husband, Steve, and I were going to try to get pregnant, and I said I knew it would take a while, because I was kind of old, and I'd probably have to do fertility treatments and all that. Well, six voices in unison, with these incredible Southern accents, all shouted, "Bull---!" They just jumped on me and said, "Why are you looking at it so pathologically?" And they were right. By the next Supper Club, I was pregnant.

It's a supportive group, but we do not coddle each other. You can't take yourself too seriously with this crowd, because we will tease you mercilessly. My mother used to say, "You only tease the people you really love."

One of us was a very high-ranking person at CARE, the international charity. One month we were at Supper Club and she said she couldn't imagine a better job. The very next month she had just come back from a business trip to Africa, which had been pivotal for her, and she was in tears on my couch, saying she didn't want her job anymore and she wanted to move to Bend, Oregon, of all places. She just picked Bend out of the blue, or her hair stylist told her about it or something.

97

And sure enough, she's in Bend now. She resigned, she sold her house, she sold just about everything she owned, and she and her dog Scout moved out to Bend to start a new life.

We call that the "Power of Supper Club." There's a stupid hand signal we do, like the international symbol for the Power of Supper Club or a secret handshake. Very tongue in cheek, of course, but there's no denying that some powerful things happen when we're all behind each other. It's this incredible voodoo of these women that makes it happen.

The night they all suggested to me that I could change my life by selling my half of my ad agency, I can't over-estimate how important that moment was for me. It literally changed my life. I was feeling very strongly that running a company and raising my baby the way I wanted to were becoming mutually exclusive, but I couldn't see a way out. I kept saying, "I own half an ad agency, I don't have any good options." This went on for months. Finally, at Supper Club, we were all sitting around on my porch drinking wine and they all said, "You own half an ad agency, you have some great options." And suddenly something clicked in my head and I realized I did. They helped me brainstorm the whole thing, right down to figuring out who could be my business partner's new business partner.

The whole group helped me see this new world of possibilities, where before I had felt completely stuck. So stuck.

And now here I am, living my dream life. I'm sitting here on my porch with my iBook, looking out at the trees, with my son sleeping upstairs.

The most important element of this group is our love for each other. Another thing is that every single one of us has a strong sense of humor. Or maybe a really low threshold for what's funny. Actually, we only have about seventeen different jokes, and we just repeat them. But seriously, the other big thing is that we are honest with each other. If someone's playing the victim, they get outed. If they're fooling themselves, we set them straight. You can't slip much by this group, because we will call you on it.

I'm not sure exactly what the magic is, but I know that pulling this group of women together is one of the best things I've done on this earth. When I'm on my deathbed, this group will be one my proudest achievements. I am so proud of each of them. Every single one of them is a remarkable woman in her own right. And when you shake them all up together in a living room with a couple of bottles of Chardonnay, watch out!

Elizabeth Cogswell Baskin,
ADVERTISING EXECUTIVE AND MOTHER

One of the world's most amazing miracles is how far our true friends will go to give us the gifts we really need. And as only our truest friends could, they often give, without being asked, the thing we most need but could never ask for.

The Secret Gift

*E*LEVEN YEARS AGO, MY MOM
WAS DIAGNOSED WITH BRAIN AND LUNG
CANCER. Needless to say, the outlook was grim. My father
was scheduled to retire that same year and my mom had
asked him to put it off due to insurance, money concerns, and
so on. So he continued working and worrying about my mom.
She had decided to undergo not only radiation treatments,
but chemotherapy as well—not a pleasant outlook either.
My partner Richard was in culinary school then, fulfilling his
lifelong dream of becoming a chef. I was working full time
at an ad agency. My only sibling also was working full time.

My brother would pick our mom up in the A.M., take
her for her radiation/chemo, and then bring her home. She
didn't want him to stay and miss work; it was her traditional

'40s upbringing. So basically, mom was left alone to endure the effects of her treatments.

She never complained. She never seemed worried. And she seemed to endure the treatments surprisingly well. Between me, my brother, and my father, we all volunteered to take time off to spend those long days with her. She wouldn't hear of it. I found that very strange.

So life went on. (If you can call it that. Losing a loved one is never life as usual.) Every day Richard would come home and I'd ask about school (not as often as I should have, given that my mind was elsewhere) and he would answer only in vague statements.

About a year later, my mom passed away. It was pretty peaceful for her, but devastating to the rest of us. About three days after she died, my partner received a small card in the mail. It was in my mom's handwriting. I freaked. "What the hell is this?" He just smiled, opened it, and started crying. He let me read it. "Thanks, Dick, for all you've done in the past year. You don't know how much that meant to me. Love, Ruth."

I finally quizzed him long enough to find out that during her time of radiation and chemotherapy, Richard had quit school; just dropped his dream. He would wait until my brother dropped my mom off in the morning from her treatments. Then he would sneak in the house and the two of them would watch the soaps, trash my sister-in-law, and pass the time.

He would run to McDonald's and pick up their shared passion of "Filet o' fish" sandwiches. Day after day. He made sure he was there to keep an eye on her and make sure she had something to do to keep her mind off her illness, as well as the effects of the treatments. They decided it would be their little secret.

I was in shock. I had never, ever had someone care about me or my family as much.

> *I was in shock. I had never ever had someone care about me or my family as much.*
>
> —ED HUERTA

And to quit school and just let go of his dream! At my mom's funeral, my father (who had become aware of what Richard had done), announced that he had a third son—Richard. And he proceeded to tell the gathering what Richard had done for my mother. It was a pretty emotional day, but I remember thinking, "This is truly my best friend!"

P.S. Three years ago, I paid for Richard to return to culinary school. He's now a chef instructor at the Greater Chicago Food Depository, helping people on welfare and other underprivileged folk enter the food service industry so they can earn a better-than-decent wage and do something they truly enjoy.

This best friend is also my partner, significant other, lover. But best friend pretty much covers it to the max.

Ed Huerta, BEST BUDDY

GOOD WILL JESTER

T look at my role {in *Good Will Hunting*} and I think that Ben {Affleck} could have easily played it. I think he let me do it because, literally, he's my best friend in the world and he's that selfless.

—*Matt Damon*, ACTOR

SOURCE: Gary Warner, *Best Friends Forever*
(White Plains: Peter Pauper Press, 2000)

At different times in our lives, we need different things from our friends. So "best friend" never really means the same thing twice in one's life. In the end, depending where you are in your life, you can have many best friends. All of them great gifts for that moment.

Better *friends*

*M*Y PARENTS ALWAYS TOLD US, "YOU DON'T HAVE 'BEST FRIENDS.'" I know it was their way of teaching us to appreciate the differences in everyone, and I think they were enlightening us to the idea that people's feelings might be at stake by references to "best" (especially the feelings of the non-"best" friend standing next to you). I did get my parents to concede to the idea of "better."

I think that "best" means different things at different points in one's life. There are childhood "best," teenage "best," young adult "best," and now-I-have-a-family (and/or husband) "best." And I'm sure there's an old-age "best."

At eight years old there was Barb Petit, a new girl in school, in my third grade class. We became best, and through us our families became best.

Barb drew horses well; I copied her horses. (Years later I found a drawing I'd done at that time. I'd drawn the hooves backward!) Barb copied the way I dressed. (And I've never been a stylish dresser—at eight years old, in 1963, it was probably my mother's stylish dressing.)

A childhood best is big. You're a kid— you've got tons of time to devote to it!

—LAURA CORNELL

With Barb I had my first sleepover. We would sneak a look at her dad's old *Playboys* (probably quite a valuable collection), which were kept on file in the stairway land- ing bookcase. Once in a while we were allowed to ride in her dad's antique Cadillac. I picture it being pink, but I think it was prob- ably just white. We had big weekend breakfasts—eggs, bacon, pancakes, conversation (she had a brother and sis- ter, and at that point my sister was coming over, too), so it was a big group in a big sunny California kitchen.

I know we spent a lot of time after school at my house, too, but I only have two big memories from my house: the chocolate milks I'd make us for snack (tons of chocolate at the bottom), and the mayonnaise jar (I'd eat a big spoonful in front of Barb to make her gag). But most of my memories are Barb's house—a big, two-story, 1920s Spanish-style house.

As we grew, we spent our time honing our sarcasm skills. We were both very sarcastic. But we used funny sarcasm, not negative sarcasm, we thought. We loved making fun of people (to each other). Everyone was a target. We spent a great deal of time in her backyard tree house, which overlooked the junior high school playing field.

We branched out in junior high. We were not so inseparable. Barb became more rebellious, aware of boys. I was not there yet. I think I bloomed late in everything.

And then in tenth grade—our first year of high school—the Petit family came to our house for dinner to break the news. They'd been transferred—they were moving. At that point, it was more the idea of life without the Petits rather than life without Barb. We wrote long letters to each other through high school and into the beginning of college. Her letters became tales of boys and smoking and alcohol—again, I was a late bloomer. Though Barb and I drifted, our families did not.

There have been other Barbs in my life. There were Cathy and Betty and Unda in junior high and high school; there was Annie in college; there was Lina in my New York single life, and Elaine in my postbaby life who, on the playground every afternoon, tolerated tales of the demise of my marriage. And there's Sally, with whom I check in regularly—brief laughs and gripes on how difficult it is to juggle everything. There's nothing like that first best, though—like going home. A childhood best is big. You're a kid—you've got tons of time to devote to it!

As a single mom who works at home, my friends are other parents. (My theory about relocation is that it's a lot easier if you have a toddler or elementary school–age child in your possession when you move.)

For a working parent (which I think is just about everyone of my generation), time is scarce. I always read about the women who talk on the phone every day to their friend of a zillion years who lives a zillion miles away. Well, my idea of a best friend is someone who has as little time to stay on the phone as I do, who never calls at dinner or bedtime, and who never has time to have lunch or coffee.

I have friends whose lives are very different from mine, but I think if I've got to put an adjective on it, a "best" for me right now is someone who shares similar trials and tribulations—and right now I guess that's a parent. Like my parents, I don't have a "best." And like my parents and the Petits, my wonderful friends now are through Lilly (my daughter!).

Laura Cornell, CHILDREN'S BOOK ILLUSTRATOR

UNPUZZLED

A friend gathers all the pieces and gives them back in the right order.

—*Toni Morrison,* WRITER

SOURCE: Angela Beasley Freeman, *100 Years of Women's Wisdom* (Nashville: Walnut Grove Press, 1999)

Being able to pare friendship down to an easy definition makes the relationships that much more meaningful. It also allows us to understand the importance of each friend in our lives. Sandy has been blessed with the gift of four special women in her life.

Defining *friendship*

I HAVE BEEN BLESSED WITH A WONDERFUL CIRCLE OF GOOD FRIENDS that I've worked with and that I've met purely socially. Of this great group of people who keep me laughing and sane, four women really stand out.

My definition of an ideal friend is a person who would do anything for you and for whom you'd do anything in return. A real test is just to see who'd drive you to the airport. That usually weeds out the true friends list pretty quickly.

I am fortunate enough to have at least four very true friends: Kathy Crowe, Joanna Halinski, Linda Johnston, and Mary Reak. They are full of love and support, and I believe would do anything for me, day or night.

Joanna is a strong woman who could change the world

if given the chance. Such energy. Such passion. She has a wonderful spirit of fun and can always make me smile. I can always count on her for a hug and a kiss and if I need to cry, she's serenely understanding. Very human.

My definition of an ideal friend is a person who would do anything for you and for whom you'd do anything in return.

—SANDY MAXX

Mary is also very strong and incredibly wise. She is very compassionate and remains close and dear to me even across the miles from Chicago to Seattle.

Linda and I built a fun friendship when we worked together in Atlanta. Her honesty and openness and joie de vivre make her a great person to be around—and again, distance does not erode our bond.

Kathy is another understanding soul with an inquisitive personality. Kathy and I can pick up a conversation after a year hiatus and talk for hours. And talk honestly. She is one of the most elegant and beautiful women I know, and she doesn't even realize her beauty.

These are four women who have enriched my life and who continue to do so. I'd do anything for each of them. I truly believe they'd do the same.

Sandy Maxx, RADIO PERSONALITY

FLAT-TIRE FRIENDS

*L*ots of people want to ride with you in the limo, but what you want is someone who will take the bus with you when the limo breaks down.

—*Oprah Winfrey,*
TV AND MEDIA PERSONALITY

SOURCE: Gary Warner, *Best Friends Forever*
(White Plains: Peter Pauper Press, 2000)

EXPLORING FRIENDSHIP

*T*here's a kind of emotional exploration you plumb with a friend that you don't really do with a family.

—*Bette Midler,* ACTRESS

SOURCE: *Friends: A Treasury of Quotations*
(Philadelphia: Running Press, 1998)

our friends are the most $\mathcal{E}$*nduring ever*

nt use will not wear

ged the fabric of friendship.

——DOROTHY PARKER

$\mathcal{L}$ife Together

I don't have friends from childhood, but I do have friends who have endured all the traumas and tribulations of adulthood. And as I go through life with these longtime friends, our relationships create a strength in me that I would not have without them.

My two closest friends have been in my life for fifteen and eight years. We endure the good and bad times.

Leslie and I met when I hired her for a graphic design project. I wanted to work with her not only because she was talented, but because I liked her. We became instant long-term friends. We laugh together, cry together, get annoyed with each other together, and in the end get support and deep love from each other. And we do it almost all on the telephone, in what seems to be one long, stream-of-consciousness, shared tale made up of everything that happens to us. We endure the fights, the joys, the breakups, the births, the firings, the ceremonies, the promotions, the wins. We endure life.

Zanne and I speak sporadically, almost always in person, almost always at a Starbucks on Manhattan's Upper West Side. But in between the coffees, when we don't see each other, we still are there for each other, going through life together. She was in Guatemala adopting her daughter the day I got married. Although we couldn't be together physically, we were together—based on the strength of a friendship that has passed the test of time.

True friendships are like riding a bike—you just never forget how to do it and no matter how long it is between bike rides, you always feel confident and free when you get back on.

The following contributors share the amazing ability of their relationships to thrive on the changes of life. This is the mystery and beauty of the long-term friendship—not easy, but then, as we've all heard since childhood, nothing worthwhile is easy.

Nothing is more genuine or more moving than the true, inexplicable, unmovable bond between two people. Even gender cannot deter friendships that are meant to last. Nicole and David's positive energy, despite some tragic times together, is a real testament to the power of friendship.

Positive *Energy*

*M*Y BEST FRIEND'S NAME
IS DAVID CLOUTIER. We've been friends since my
first week at school at UCLA. I was seventeen then and
I'm now thirty-three. We've been through everything. We
started out as college coeds and then became camp coun-
selors over the summer. Then we went on to live in a one-
room New York apartment, which was pretty hilarious.
And we've been through some tragic situations together.
We were on vacation with lots of our friends when Dave's
brother died in a tragic accident. And we got through that
together. We're used to the extremes. In recent years we've
danced at bar mitzvahs to make money. And then we used
the money we earned to go on vacation to Costa Rica
and attack the jungle. And with my recent diagnosis of an

inoperable brain tumor, Dave (and the bond between us) came through. He's the person who makes me laugh the most even in the most tragic situations. We've been through the wringer together.

David has a party business. He recruits people to get the dance floor going and to take care of the teenage kids at bar mitzvahs. To make some extra money, I'd do everything from leading the hora to dancing with Uncle Harry. And believe me, I am the token shiksa. We would get paid to get the crowd going, leading them in dance numbers by everyone from the Village People to Frank Sinatra. David and I would whisper and strategize as to which family members we could get out on the dance floor—which reluctant members we could get to dance. It was hilarious for the two of us to dance the hora and lift Grandma up in the chair. It was quite a riot.

We've had lots of fun together, but what's been so wild is that he's unconditional when life is constantly changing conditions. I mean, we've run the gamut of life's hilarious laughter—from adventures like road trips to getting through bad things like funerals and my brain tumor.

When I got diagnosed with my brain tumor, which was exactly one year ago, they told me I had three to six months to live. My parents and my siblings were in my hospital room and the phone calls and the tears and the flowers kept coming. Well, in walks Dave, who happened to be in the area. The room looks like a funeral parlor, and the mood is as thick as you can imagine. And he doesn't say much, just hugs everybody.

Well, they leave and all he says to me is, "I bought princess movies." Nothing about the tumor. And I said, "You what?" And he repeated, "I bought princess movies." And I open the bag and there's three movies: *Shakespeare in Love*, *The Princess Bride*, and *Ever After*. And he says, "I want you to feel like a princess." We didn't mention the tumor or that I could have only a few months to live.

> *Everyone had told us you should always date your friend, so we tried, but we like being best friends. He's a hoot.*
>
> —NICOLE VON RUDEN

Here was this person who knew exactly what I needed. It was the most awesome and unique gift. And I'm sitting there unbelievably, totally overwhelmed by what life has brought me, and in walks this funny person. And the amazing thing is that it's not like we had any history of those movies; he just knew the perfect thing to do. It was a sweet, sweet thing.

Dave is one of three boys and we were all on vacation together when his youngest brother had a freak accident and fell to his death. It was really terrible. We got through that together in an amazing way. I flew home with him and was with Dave when he told his mom.

This is the person who is by far and away the most hilarious person in my life. If anybody has provided the most therapeutic laughter, it's Dave. And it's amazing because people can tend to get bitter when these things happen in their lives, but not Dave. The neatest thing is that he can make you laugh during tragic situations or amidst life situations. We are completely able to share our wildest emotions together and we also know when we need to sit quietly.

We tried dating for about eight weeks. And we both looked at each other and went no, no let's go back to being friends. It was never awkward after that. Everyone had told us you should always date your friend, so we tried, but we like being best friends. He's a hoot.

Nicole von Ruden, TEACHER

Beyond Best *friends*

*W*E HAVE A GOOD FRIEND-
SHIP. We met so long ago and have followed each
other throughout our lives. She has such a positive
energy about her and I'm attracted to people, guys and
girls, who are very much like me—very positive. That's
how it started. We met each other the first day at
UCLA and we just did
everything together; we
worked together, we went
to school together—we
were best friends. She was
someone I could always
consult with about any-
thing. We kept it on a
friends level pretty much the whole time. Once we
tried dating—sort of—and had a falling out. The hard-
est thing about dating a best friend, someone you're
that close to, is that it is hard for things to change. You
are already so close and you do everything and talk
about everything together—and once you're officially

> *W*e'll never have to
> worry about the arguments
> couples have.
>
> —DAVE CLOUTIER

dating you want more, but there really isn't any more to give or get; you already know everything about each other. There is no discovery process. We are much better friends than we were lovers.

Even when we've had times when we haven't actually talked to each other for a couple of months, we can pick up where we left off. There are times that we have talked every day, sometimes more than once a day, and then not spoken again for weeks. But no matter how long between phone calls, we are always there for each other.

I started this party business about thirteen years ago. It's about creating positive energy and good times at the events. She was a perfect fit. She has a great personality, she is extremely vivacious, and I think that people tend to flock to people like her. She really got those parties going. If I had just two more Nicoles working for me, I would be a very lucky employer!

We once lived together in a *very* small apartment in New York. That is where our relationship really began to evolve. We had just worked together at a summer camp, but now we were forced to deal with each other's every mood. In a situation like that, you get to know who that person really is—the real essence of the person. Nicole has such wonderful energy. It's magnetic. And she's always so truthful with me. It made New York less scary for me knowing that she was there. And living together . . . all barriers were broken down, and physical appearances no longer mattered. You get so beyond that. That really strengthened our friendship. Now I can't go to New York without being reminded of experiences we shared.

Dates get jealous—a lot. They were very envious of the relationship I have with her. (There would have been no problem had she been a guy!) But our friendship is very special; it doesn't happen every day. And to make matters worse, our parents kept trying to pair us up. They couldn't understand how we could have such a close relationship and not be lovers. But it's better the way things are because we'll never have to worry about the arguments couples have. I can call Nicole when I have a problem or when I have a question. It's nice to have someone always there. Even for simple things. I'm driving and I see something that reminds me of something we've shared or I think that she'd find funny, so I call her and say, "You wouldn't believe what I just saw . . ." and we laugh. And that's all I say, it's the whole conversation.

> *I can call Nicole when I have a problem, when I have a question. It's nice to have someone always there.*
>
> —DAVE CLOUTIER

And that's Nicole. I think those moments are really very special.

Nic was recently diagnosed with an inoperable brain tumor. I was terrified. It never occurred to me that I could lose her. I just happened to be visiting her when the doctors gave her that horrible "time limit." How can they really know how long a person will live? I feel very fortunate that I was there for her that day. It was so tough; and she really needed someone outside her family. And yet . . . I could not let her know that I was terrified because she needed to know that she could fight it. And as scared as I was, I believed she could fight it. I always got the feeling that she looked to me for guidance, and I wasn't going to let her down. It sounds kind of hokey, but I really wanted to be the strong shoulder for her. If the roles were reversed, I have no doubt that she would do the same for me.

This whole ordeal has really shown me how important her relationship is to me. We have been through so much together that the tumor has just become another chapter in the story of our friendship. I cannot imagine what my life would have been like had we never met. The laughs, the adventures, and the tears—lucky for me, for us, we'll never have to find that out. I love you, Nic.

David Cloutier, PARTY PLANNER

LISTEN, LISTEN, LISTEN

*T*he most called upon requisite of a friend is an accessible ear.

—*Maya Angelou,* POET

SOURCE: Angela Beasley Freeman, *100 Years of Women's Wisdom* (Nashville: Walnut Grove Press, 1999)

Pen pals provide us with a great way to learn about other cultures and worlds—and also to make a friend. Mary Catherine met her friend Janette through a series of letters, and finally managed to meet her more than twenty years after their correspondence started.

A Magna Carta *f*riend

*W*HEN I WAS LITTLE, I USED TO DREAM OF TRAVELING AND LIVING IN DIFFERENT COUNTRIES. I wondered what the people looked like, what their concerns were, what games they played. I used to spin the globe and let my finger decide where I would live my life.

A young girl in Motherwell, Scotland, had an assignment in school to take a pen, close her eyes, and touch the pen to a map of the world. The student was then to write the local newspaper, asking to find her a pen pal from wherever the pen had landed, and also asking to please publish the letter.

Popeidia Nedelkoff, our priest's wife and a staff member at the *Fort Wayne Journal Gazette*, thought of me when she received a letter from a Janette Easton of Motherwell, Scotland, looking for an American pen pal from Fort Wayne, Indiana, of all places.

Janette and I began writing when we were both eight years old. We are both Cancers, both left-handed, and both have one sibling in the form of an older brother. Our letters were frequent throughout childhood and high school, less frequent while we were in college. Janette studied social care and health care at a local college in Motherwell. I studied business, French, and art in Houston, quite a ways from home. We lost contact in our early twenties, due mostly to my nomadic nature. Janette wrote to my parents after a few years, and our letters began again. As adults we wrote about changes in our lives, our families, new nieces and nephews on her part, new travels on my part, job traumas, and men troubles. I began to wonder: Who was this woman I had been writing to all of these years? What did she look like? What indeed did Motherwell, Scotland, look like?

In March 1990, I participated in a exhibition in

> *After twenty-one years of writing, I finally met Janette and her family.*
>
> —MARY CATHERINE ROTH

London. I contacted Janette and we planned that I would come to Motherwell to meet her during my trip. It was the first time we had ever spoken on the telephone. Excitement was in both of our voices. After twenty-one years of writing, I finally met Janette and her family. She had the first letter I had sent her, with my picture at eight years old. We laughed and we cried. We went out dancing and sightseeing and basically had a ball. After all those years of writing, I found out that Magna Carta Street, to which I had been addressing the letters, was really Magna Street. Janette had thought about correcting me, but both she and the postman thought it was funny. Janette came to London the following weekend to tool around the city with me and see my exhibition.

I had been to Scotland once before and had tried to locate Motherwell, but did not succeed. I loved Scotland on my first trip, and even more so on my second trip. Motherwell is a small industrial town with down-to-earth people. I loved my visit and meeting my special friend and her family, my pen pal for life, Janette Easton. I hope in the near future, Janette will visit me in New York, Fort Wayne, or wherever I may be.

Mary Catherine Roth, ARTIST

Sometimes we start as enemies—but we're really meant to be friends. Rachel and her friend Andrea were wary of each other at first, when they met as eight-year-olds. After clicking over a teen idol, however, they formed a friendship that has lasted their whole lives.

We Won't
*G*row Up

I MET MY FIRST BEST FRIEND
WHEN I WAS JUST EIGHT. It was sort of a "blind date"—you see, my great aunt Molly was the secretary to her father, a famous doctor. It was hate at first sight. We were determined not to let this match occur. I first set eyes on her at Knights Day Camp ("Come now and sing our song") where she was holding court to a group of eager seven-year-olds. She was lecturing them from a stage! How dare she, I thought, steal my stage, bask in my glory? *I* was the only eight-year-old allowed to hold a captive audience—who did she think she was? (Obviously, she didn't know who she was dealing with.)

We met again four years later in sixth grade. I had heard through the prepubescent grapevine that she was changing schools. Hah, I thought, now she's on *my* territory. No chance for her survival in the dog-eat-dog world of a private girls' school. And besides, facts being facts, I was a blonde. She was not.

We avoided each other like the plague for three whole days, and then the circling began. My soldiers were lined up behind their mascot, but she, too, had her powers—there were other new girls in town. On day five our paths crossed by our lockers. I had my full-length portrait of Bobby Sherman cemented to my locker, and she proceeded to put up her own poster of . . . Davey Jones. Could it be—she liked the Monkees? Maybe she was okay?

I love having wonderful female friendships—to me they're as important as the air I breathe.

—RACHEL SUSSMAN

"So you like the Monkees?" I asked tentatively.

"Yeah, they're okay, but the Beatles are cooler. I also like the J. Geils Band."

That was it. We were in love. We were inseparable all through school (except for the one year that we didn't speak). We are still great friends today, although the continental United States keeps us apart, and she is the only professional woman I know who can't master e-mail. But, most importantly, whenever we see each other, we're still Rachel and Andrea, the hysterically laughing thirteen-year-olds.

Oh, I've had other best friends—great friends, brilliant friends, funny and wacky friends. Some friendships have lasted almost a lifetime, and some were longer or shorter than they should have been. Friends can bring great joy and pain, but I wouldn't give up good friendships for anything. I love having wonderful female friendships—to me they're as important as the air I breathe.

Rachel Sussman, PSYCHOTHERAPIST

STRINGING ALONG

*I*t wasn't until an uncle of mine emigrated to Canada, leaving behind an old Spanish guitar with five rusty strings, that my enormous and clumsy fingers found a musical home, and I found what was to be my best friend.

—*Sting,* MUSICIAN

SOURCE: Gary Warner, *Best Friends Forever*
(White Plains: Peter Pauper Press, 2000)

*A*cross the street or across the *world*—your friends are there no matter where you want to go. Salli and a girlfriend took a cross-country trip in college, and she and her friends have been traveling together ever since, no matter what else has happened in their lives.

Traveling *C*ompanions

*T*RUE FRIENDS ARE THERE NO MATTER WHAT. You can always pick up where you left off.

I have these two friends—Donna and Jennifer. Donna I've known since I was eight; Jennifer since I was six. We all grew up in Ridgefield, Connecticut, and we really shared our childhood and adolescence. These are the girls in high school that you can turn to and say, "Let's take off and do a ski weekend." These are my friends who really know me.

In 1979, Donna and I set out to do a trip across the country. Our whole lives we had talked about it—taking off and seeing the United States. We talked at the end of our sophomore year in college, and one of us said, "You know what—we should take a year off and go cross country." Both of our parents were ready to shoot us. Donna had this new little Renault, and on September 15 we left and worked our way across the country. We weren't even twenty-one—we were hardly legal. We found ourselves everywhere from Florida to New Orleans to the Grand Canyon. Anyone we knew across the country, we basically drove to their house and stayed with them. We had the greatest experience together. We landed in Aspen, Colorado, at the end of November. Three days after we got there, our car was totaled by a drunken driver. We were stuck there, so we got jobs with the Aspen Ski Corps and we also got night jobs. We had free ski passes, and did a lot of great partying.

Donna was the girl who never settled down and was always floating around. I went back to college. Through the years we stuck together. I had another pivotal point with her. In 1985 she took a job in Europe with a ski magazine in sales. She had to travel to ski resorts all over Europe. I took three weeks off from my job and went to visit her with another friend. We skied all over Europe. I came back and broke up with my boyfriend; Annie, the friend I went with, got divorced; and Donna came back to the United States. We all settled in an apartment in Boston together.

We have been together in all parts of the world. Anywhere I've ever lived, we've visited each other. Just recently Donna, Jennifer, and Annie and I all went out to Colorado for the weekend. No husbands, no children. We just had this great girls' weekend. We ate, spa-ed, and talked—I've known these women for thirty-five years of my life. In the business I'm in, it can be so fake and phony. I found it to be a very soul-searching type of weekend. These are friends you can do anything in front of. You can say anything. You can talk about sex, marriage, any-thing. I felt really at peace with myself. It was really nice to be me. I'm happy to have those kinds of connections. I'm around a lot of tragedy right now—divorce, deaths— and you realize how few people will be there for you. When I look at these three women, I say, these are my unconditional friends. They provide me with uncondi-tional love and friendship even though they don't live near me. You just don't get that anywhere. Thank God for e-mail.

> *These are friends you can do anything in front of. You can say anything. You can talk about sex, marriage, anything.*
>
> —SALLI HESS

Salli Hess, TELEVISION EXECUTIVE

FOREVER

*C*hildren grow and go; even beloved men sometimes seem to be beaming their perceptions and responses in from a different planet. But our female friends are forever.

—*Anna Quindlen,* AUTHOR

SOURCE: Helen Moore, compiler, *A Friend for all Seasons* (White Plains: Peter Pauper Press, 1998)

The best friends are often the ones who grow and change with you, who experience the same things in their lives that you do, and who are there for you no matter what.

My *Girlies*

*W*E ALL CAME FROM DIFFERENT
PARTS OF THE CITY. It was the summer of 1981
and little did we know that when we met at college in
Binghamton, New York, we would be forming friendships
that would last forever and, hopefully, a day.

None of us entered college with a whole lot of money.
Nor did we all come from families that totally understood
the collegiate life—especially the fact that we would not
be living at home. Nevertheless, we prevailed. Not neces-
sarily finishing at the same time or at the same school,
but finishing.

In the interim, we learned from one another. We understood that hard work would allow us to accomplish our
goals. We knew that there was more to life than the

neighborhoods or even the city where we came from. And we all agreed that having fun and playing with boys was cool, too.

One of the initial things that began our bonding process was our determination to reach the outer limits. We all took turns, either with one another or with other friends, and back-packed through Europe. During the planning stages, we would share information with the others on our experiences. Before you knew it, we had all gone to Europe and had a fabulous time there. This is when our passion for traveling and exploring different places began.

> *We are enjoying life or choosing to just simply take it easy; however, we have never forgotten each other. We continue to grow in different ways but always together in our hearts*
>
> —BELBELIN MOJICA

The next thing that bought us together was our determination to develop professions for ourselves. We understand the value of succeeding. That being poor is tolerable, but having money is better. We knew that hard work and making money would allow us such things as a good education for our children, the ability to purchase a home, and travel. As one of my friends said, "You can take my house, you can take my children, but do not, and I mean do not, take my vacations away!"

Now we are all sort of grown up. We now have parents that we need to look after and have experienced the pain of having loved ones pass away. We have gone through the processes of school, working, dating, marriage, and children. We are enjoying life or choosing to just simply take it easy; however, we have never forgotten each other. We continue to grow in different ways but always together in our hearts.

When my dad passed away two years ago, I reconfirmed how fortunate I am to have friends like these. I basically grew up an only child. But my friends Carmentica, Elizabeth, Lisette, Sheila, and Suzette were there not just for a few hours or for a day, but throughout the entire grieving process. As I reminisce back to the day my father was buried, I recall all those that were sitting at my mother's living room—and they included my girlies.

Belbelin Mojica, EDUCATION PROGRAMS
MANAGER, THE METROPOLITAN MUSEUM OF ART